Girls Play to Win

CHEERLEADING

by Marty Gitlin

Content Consultant
Tami Krause

Head Coach/Coordinator
Minnesota Vikings Cheerleaders
and the Minnesota Swarm
Performance Team

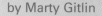
NORWOOD HOUSE PRESS
CHICAGO, ILLINOIS

Norwood House Press
P.O. Box 316598
Chicago, Illinois 60631

For information regarding Norwood House Press, please visit our website at
www.norwoodhousepress.com or call 866-565-2900.

Editor: Chrös McDougall
Designer: Christa Schneider
Project Management: Red Line Editorial

Library of Congress Cataloging-in-Publication Data

Gitlin, Marty.
 Girls play to win cheerleading / by Marty Gitlin.
    p. cm. -- (Girls play to win)
 Includes bibliographical references and index.
 Summary: "Covers the history, rules, fundamentals, and significant
personalities of the sport of women's cheerleading. Topics include:
techniques, strategies, competitive events, and equipment. Glossary,
Additional Resources, and Index included"--Provided by publisher.
 ISBN-13: 978-1-59953-462-6 (library edition : alk. paper)
 ISBN-10: 1-59953-462-2 (library edition : alk. paper)
 1. Cheerleading--Juvenile literature. I. Title.
 LB3635.G58 2011
 791.6'4--dc22
                            2011011035

Manufactured in the United States of America in North Mankato, Minnesota.
198R—032012

Girls Play to Win
CHEERLEADING

Table of Contents

Words in **bold type** are defined in the glossary.

▲ These Ben-Gals cheerleaders dance to fire up the home crowd during a Cincinnati Bengals professional football game in 2010.

CHAPTER 1

CHEERLEADING
BASICS

Cheerleading is so much more than leading **cheers**. To millions of women, girls, and even young men, it's competition. It's gymnastics. It's exercise. It's pride and self-respect. Just ask Laura Vikmanis and her daughters.

In 2008, Vikmanis was almost 40 years old and not feeling as healthy as she would have liked. She tried vari-

Beginning to Cheer

It takes commitment to become an accomplished cheerleader. It also requires a financial and time investment. Those who want to take up the activity must first decide to put in the work. Many young prospects attend local sporting events that feature cheerleaders. There they can study the cheerleaders. If they decide they want to cheer, the next step is taking lessons or joining a team. Formal and structured cheerleading classes can be found anywhere in the country.

ous activities. But it was not until she attended a National Football League (NFL) game featuring the local Cincinnati Bengals that she found one. She was particularly interested in the Ben-Gals, the team's cheerleaders.

Vikmanis tried out for the squad but did not make the cut. She felt intimidated knowing that the Ben-Gals were all about half her age. But she refused to give up. She worked on her fitness and tried out again the next year. And this time she made it. She was the only 40-year-old cheerleader in the NFL. Soon she experienced the thrill of cheering in front of 65,000 fans.

Perhaps her biggest fans were her 13-year-old and 11-year-old daughters, who were both competitive cheerleaders themselves. "I look at myself as a role model for my children to show them that no matter what age or what dream you have, you can work really hard and achieve it," Vikmanis said.

GETTING STARTED

Many people identify cheerleaders as people who do just that: lead cheers. And for more than 100 years, they have! Cheerleaders bring spirit and energy to thousands of youth, high school, college, and professional sporting events every year. These days, however, many cheerleaders have taken to competing themselves.

Competitive cheerleading mixes elements of dance, gymnastics, and traditional cheerleading. At a competition, cheerleading teams representing a school or an independent club perform high-energy, acrobatic **routines** while an upbeat song plays. Like traditional cheerleaders, competitive cheerleaders often use their voices to chant and their arms, legs, and hands for **motions**. They sometimes even use props such as **pompoms**, **megaphones**, hand-held signs, or flags during their routine. They also perform dance moves. Starting with higher levels, such as high school, more advanced cheerleaders motivate and entertain crowds through gymnastic moves such as **tumbling passes**, cartwheels, and **stunts**. The goal is to perform an exciting routine with synchronized movements, breathtaking acrobatics, and a lot of energy.

Many organizations run cheerleading competitions, and those competitions often have several different divisions within them. Some of the teams are only for girls. Others are coed, meaning they have both boys and girls.

All Star cheerleaders compete as independent teams rather than cheering for other teams.

ALL STARS

As competitive cheerleading grew in popularity during the late-1980s and 1990s, All Star cheerleading emerged as an alternative to traditional school-based cheerleading teams. All Star cheer programs are run as a separate business, similar to a dance studio or a gym. They don't cheer for other teams; they only compete. In fact, many All Star teams are made up of students from various schools in a given area.

All Star cheerleading involves choreographed routines that include dancing, tumbling, and stunting to music. Depending on the organization and division in which a team competes, teams can be coed or girls-only. All Star teams compete at various levels, with some cheerleaders beginning as early as age six. Many All Star teams train together year-round.

▲ *University of Alabama cheerleaders root for their Crimson Tide football team during a 2010 game.*

Cheerleaders come from all different backgrounds. Some start cheerleading at early ages through youth squads or by attending camps. Others join a team in high school or even in college after a career in dance or gymnastics. No matter how a team comes together, the members often spend a lot of time together at practices and become great friends. And there is nothing like performing in front of thousands of people at a sporting event or competition!

LEARNING THE BASICS

Four of the primary functions beginning cheerleaders must learn are motions, chants, **cheers,** and **jumps**. Then they might progress into tumbling, dance, and stunting.

Motions are performed with the arms and legs. They are critical to learning cheerleading because chants and cheers are performed while executing a series of motions. And they are best practiced in front of a mirror. Arm lines, technique, and angles are very important.

Arm motions must be executed in a sharp and precise manner. Such movements are thrusts made by the arm in certain directions with various hand placements. There are not as many leg motions. But they must also be done with precision. Performing leg motions at the same time as arm movements requires solid concentration and physical coordination.

A chant is a combination of words and motions. Timing is essential to a proper chant. The goal is to motivate fans to chant along with the cheerleader. To achieve that goal, the cheerleader repeats the chant in front of the crowd. Chants must also be memorized. Young cheerleaders might struggle with proper motion if they are trying to remember a chant at the same time.

Doing a "Bucket"

One of many basic hand motions is called a *bucket*. Why? Because the hand is held in a fist, as if it was holding a bucket handle. To perform a bucket motion, hold your arm and wrist straight and firm. Make a fist with the back of your hand facing up.

The same holds true for cheers. They are longer than chants but not repeated. The intention of a cheer is to motivate the team and also to urge fans to cheer. They too must be timed well with arm and leg motions.

Jumps are done more to entertain than to engage the crowd. They take a lot of practice and should not be used in public until mastered. A successful jump requires four steps done properly: Preparation, lift, execution, and landing. They are often performed to celebrate a good play in the game, such as a touchdown in football. Specific movements, chants, cheers, and jumps are learned over time.

Cheerleading Camps

Cheerleading camps can be fun. Some require that students stay overnight or spend days at a time. Many advanced teams will spend a few days in the summer choreographing their routine or routines for the year. However, you should probably have some experience before committing to a cheerleading camp. Camps can be far more expensive and time consuming than cheerleading classes. Many young cheerleading students also take lessons in gymnastics and dance. Becoming limber is critical to success as a cheerleader. Gymnastics skills can also be very useful at more advanced levels of cheerleading.

THE COMPETITIVE TEAM

When a cheerleader masters advanced routines, she is often ready to join a competitive team. Hundreds of high school and college squads throughout the country compete in dozens of local, regional, and national events. One of their tasks can be to perform stunts, which can be quite complex and difficult.

Competitive squads include the following positions:

Bases: These team members provide a foundation for any stunt. They are responsible for keeping steady those who perform in the air. It is essential for bases to have strong arms and shoulders so they can stay in control. Bases must be balanced so **flyers** and tumblers don't fall. One slip by a base often causes

Cheerleaders use equipment such as megaphones and pompoms to help encourage fans.

POMPOMS OR POMPONS?

A debate has been waged in recent years. The question? What is the spelling of the fluff ball used by cheerleaders? The word pompons *comes from the French language, but many Americans have adapted the name to be "pompoms." Those are not the only two spellings that have been used for the cheerleading tool. Others break it up into two words and refer to them as "pom poms" or "pom pons." Some even use hyphens and refer to them as "pom-poms" or "pom-pons." Today, many people simply call them "poms."*

▲ *Flyers perform some of the most exciting cheerleading moves, but also some of the most difficult ones.*

the entire stunt to collapse. Timing and teamwork are essential characteristics for a base.

Tumblers: The top gymnasts on a competitive cheerleading team generally take on this role. Tumblers bring style and entertainment to the routine. They often do handsprings and cartwheels, round-offs, and **tucks** while their teammates perform stunts. Tumblers must remain sharp and display energy to put on a good show.

Flyers: These are generally the smallest and lightest members of a competitive team. That makes them easier to lift and to be thrown and caught. Flyers are acrobatic and always are aware of where their arms and legs are as they perform their routines. But they must also display confidence and poise. They can't appear nervous as they ascend to the top of a **pyramid**. That costs the team points. Flyers must have great confidence in their base and great balance and control.

Back Spotter: Flyers depend on the back spotter to keep them safe. Stunts such as pyramids can be quite dangerous. That is especially true when the flyers are being tossed into the air. The back spotter must understand the routines well enough to know their most dangerous points. She also must be strong and quick so she can catch flyers before they hit the ground. Spotters must use good technique when catching or guiding teammates out of the **cradle** in order to prevent injuries.

HOW THEY ARE JUDGED

A group of trained eyes are watching every move a competitive cheerleading team makes. Those eyes belong to the judges.

Different competitions feature various scoring systems. The scoring most often used allows a maximum of 100 points. Teams are judged in the following categories:

Jumps and Stunts: The judges evaluate the level of performance in the routines in this category.

Proper technique: The judges are looking for the athletes not just to do the moves or skills, but to do them safely and with the correct form.

Spirit: The ability to put on an entertaining performance with personality and showmanship.

Difficulty: Teams earn more points based on handling tougher stunts and displaying a range of talents.

Choreography: The creativity, sharpness, and timing of the routines and the shifts from one stunt to another are judged in this category.

Overall Effectiveness: The team is judged by how well it performs all the skills required in the competition. Creativity and energy are also evaluated.

THE VALUE OF COMPETITION

Not all cheerleaders and dancers can perform on winning teams. But many believe competing and participating in those activities can provide life lessons. Among them is Linda Rae Chappell. She gave the following advice to her fellow cheerleading coaches:

> *Keep in mind that each practice, each performance, and each experience in front of the judges can help prepare your squad members for life's challenges in adult circumstances. . . . Your role should always be to reinforce lifetime values, choices, and skills. True winning is not determined by a score sheet, a trophy, or a photograph in a newspaper. The real winners show grace in victory, poise and perseverance in defeat.*

▲ *The emergence of competitive cheerleading has taken the sport to new heights.*

▲ *A University of Minnesota cheerleader riles up a crowd. Minnesota had the first on-field cheerleader in 1889.*

CHAPTER 2

RAH, RAH, RAH!

Fans attending Princeton University football games for the first time in the 1880s were in for a shock. As they watched the Tigers play, the fans heard a chant coming from the stands.

"RAH, RAH, RAY! TIGER, TIGER, SIS, SIS, SIS! BOOM, BOOM, BOOM. AAAAAH! PRINCETON, PRINCETON, PRINCETON!"

The unusual chant was coming from members of the **pep club** at the prestigious New Jersey school. In 1884, a Princeton graduate named Thomas Peebles moved to Minneapolis, Minnesota. He introduced University of Minnesota students to pep clubs and the chants he had learned back at Princeton.

Two students embraced the concept of leading cheers. They were rugby players John W. Adams and Win Sargent. Together they created a chant to motivate their teammates. Their battle cry was "SKI-U-MAH!" They reasoned that "SKI" was a Native American term meaning "victory" and "U-MAH" rhymed with "RAH, RAH!"

By the end of the decade, pep clubs, cheers, and even "fight songs" had become popular. Fight songs are school-specific songs that are played by pep bands and sung by students at college sporting events. They could be heard at football games at many colleges by 1890. But the University of Minnesota can still take credit for the creation of the on-field cheerleader.

The Minnesota Golden Gophers football team was struggling in October 1889. It had lost three straight games. The school newspaper urged students to attend the last game of the season. A group of male students had been chosen to lead the cheers. The fans were strongly encouraged to follow their lead.

▲ *Famous radio personality Kay Kyser (right) and a male cheerleader cheer for the University of North Carolina football team during a 1939 game against rival Duke University.*

One of the "yell leaders" was Johnny Campbell. He was inspired to pick up a megaphone and race to the edge of the field. He screamed out chants such as:

"RAH, RAH, RAH! SKI-U-MAH, HOO-RAH! HOO-RAH! VARSITY! VARSITY! VARSITY! MINNESOTA!"

Campbell was credited with being the first cheerleader. He also helped inspire the Gophers to victory.

GROWTH OF SPORTS, GROWTH OF CHEERLEADING

The growth of cheerleading mirrored that of sports such as football and basketball. Its popularity grew with the invention of basketball in 1891. Cheerleading and cheering along were considered natural and fun forms of expressing a rooting interest for a team. Soon new techniques and skills were added. Those new methods of cheerleading were refined over the years.

But one major difference would have to wait until the 1920s. Until that decade, cheerleaders were all male. And once again, the University of Minnesota took the lead in changing the landscape. In 1923, the school introduced the first female cheerleaders at its sporting events. It took many years for cheerleading to become primarily led by women. But the seeds had been planted.

Negative opinions of cheerleaders began to emerge early in the 20th century. Authors Natalie Guice-Adams and Pamela Bettis explained those feelings in their 2003 book titled *Cheerleader! An American Icon*:

Tragic End

Many knew Johnny Campbell as the Father of Cheerleading. But he didn't live to see the activity he started flourish. Cheerleading became tremendously popular in the 1950s, but he was gone well before that. Campbell was killed in a car accident in 1936. He was driving in a blizzard in Minnesota when the accident occurred.

In 1911, when all cheer leaders or yell leaders were males, the president of Harvard University attacked "organized cheering" as a deplorable avenue for college men to express emotion, and contended that this new college tradition offered nothing of value to respectable educated men. This attack did not keep the activity from growing, and by the 1920s, cheerleaders on college campuses were highly respected.

The arrival of women brought a new style to cheerleading. Tumbling and other gymnastics routines became more commonly used. Soon cheerleading was introduced into U.S. high schools. However, most of the tumbling and gymnastics was done by men.

During the next decade, some cheerleaders began using pompoms made of wool or crepe paper in their routines. Cheerleaders believed the brightly colored

"Just Yells"

The first instructional book about cheerleading was published in 1927. It was titled *Just Yells: A Guide for Cheerleaders*. Author Willis Bugbee wrote many books in the first half of the 20th century. Several of them had far more colorful titles. Included were *Uncle Si and the Sunbeam Club*, *Happyville School Picnic*, *Closing Day at Beanville Schools*, and *Aunt Sophronia at College*.

▲ *These University of Nebraska cheerleaders pose around 1929. They led cheers at Cornhuskers football games.*

pompoms, which were also called "shakeroos," made them stand out more. After all, they were often doing their routines quite far from many of the spectators. They were particularly distant at football games.

U.S. participation in World War II began in 1941 and signaled the end of male majority in cheerleading. Many high school boys lost interest in the activity. And millions of college-age men left school to fight overseas. That left girls and young women to take over the cheerleading squads.

By the end of the war, an estimated 90 percent of all cheerleaders were female. They have dominated the activity ever since. That is especially true at the youth, middle school, and high school levels.

President George W. Bush was a cheerleader at Phillips Academy during the 1960s.

THEY WERE ALL CHEERLEADERS!

Some of the most famous people in the United States were cheerleaders, including four presidents: Franklin D. Roosevelt, Dwight Eisenhower, Ronald Reagan, and George W. Bush. Others in the political world who led cheers were Supreme Court Justice Ruth Bader Ginsburg and Senators Trent Lott and Thad Cochran.

Noted actresses who led cheers in their youth were Courteney Cox, Teri Hatcher, Reese Witherspoon, Cameron Diaz, Sandra Bullock, Halle Berry, Renee Zellweger, Blake Lively, Meryl Streep, and Sally Field. Celebrated leading men such as Jimmy Stewart and Samuel L. Jackson spent time as cheerleaders. So did comedians Jerry Lewis and Steve Martin. CBS news anchor Katie Couric was a cheerleader. Singers Madonna, Miley Cyrus, Faith Hill, Toni Basil, Christina Aguilera, Carrie Underwood, and Lauryn Hill once cheered as well.

LAWRENCE 'HERKIE' HERKIMER

A man named Lawrence "Herkie" Herkimer was most responsible for cheerleading exploding in popularity. The Texan embraced the activity during his teenage years at North Dallas High School and later at Southern Methodist University (SMU).

During his time at SMU, he created what became known as the "Herkie Jump." While leaping in the air, he threw his right arm straight up and placed his left arm on his hip. He kicked his left leg straight out and his right leg back. The jump became adopted around the cheerleading world as the signature ending to a routine. But what many didn't know about the "Herkie Jump" was that Herkimer invented it by accident.

"It was just a poor split jump," he admitted. "I don't like to tell people that."

Herkimer's influence extended far beyond his famous jump. In 1946 and 1947, he was asked to conduct cheerleading clinics at Sam Houston State University in Texas. The following year he founded the National Cheerleading Association (NCA). The NCA camps, which were also held in Texas, proved to be a rousing success.

The first camp, however, attracted just 52 participants. It featured a speech professor providing instruction on how to speak in front of crowds. It also included an English teacher giving advice on rhyming cheers.

Wealthy and Fit

Lawrence "Herkie" Herkimer got quite rich from launching his cheerleading camp empire. He sold his business for $20 million in 1986. Then he purchased a 6,000-square-foot beach home in Florida.

The *New York Times* reported in 2009 that the 83-year-old Herkimer still exercised three days a week at a fitness club. He was also playing golf three days a week. But he was no longer doing his famous "Herkie Jump."

But only Herkimer captured the attention of the students and brought out their enthusiasm. His gymnastics moves and sharp motions showed them how to excite and engage fans.

The students returned home and passed the word about the new NCA camp. The following year 350 signed up. Within a few years, 20,000 cheerleaders were attending NCA camps.

The popularity of cheerleading was about to explode. But it would take quite some time before it blossomed into a competitive activity.

▲ *This art student paints a large megaphone for the cheerleaders at her Washington D.C. high school during the 1940s.*

▲ Cheerleaders from Radcliffe College cheer on the Boston Patriots pro football team in 1965.

CHAPTER 3

"BIG SKIRTS AND POMPOMS"

The image most people have of cheerleaders began to form during the 1950s. In high schools throughout the United States, girls led cheers on the sidelines for their football and basketball teams.

There were some major differences from today's sport. For one, cheerleading outfits covered more of the body back then. Tatsumi Johnson, the owner and program director of the California Cheer Gym, spoke about the image and motivation of cheerleaders from that era.

"Big skirts and pompoms," she said. "Cheerleaders reached new heights in the 1950s. They became very popular because they thought it was a very exciting thing to support their male athletes in all sports. The way they were chosen was by the student body with their smiles or popularity."

Cheering for "Pop"

The Pop Warner Football organization had become quite popular throughout the country by the 1960s. By the end of the decade, it boasted more than 3,000 youth football teams. But football was for boys. Girls felt like they were being left out in the cold. Many of them had brothers who played Pop Warner football. They did not feel involved simply cheering from the stands. They yearned to share in the excitement down on the field.

So Pop Warner gave them a chance. The new Pop Warner cheerleading activity grew in popularity in the 1970s. Today, an estimated 180,000 girls are participating in what is now known as the Pop Warner Spirit Program. Pop Warner offers an opportunity for girls to learn cheerleading during the football season or year-round. The organization also runs cheerleading competitions.

Going Pro

In 1954, cheerleading took another historic step. That year, the Baltimore Colts of the National Football League (NFL) became the first professional sports team to hire cheerleaders. The trend continued throughout the 1960s. Nearly every NFL team and all National Basketball Association (NBA) teams now feature cheerleaders.

That was not always the case. In 1955, Newark High School in Delaware listed "desirable traits for cheerleaders." Among them were "good manners, responsibility, dependability, leadership ability, [good grades], and citizenship of high standing."

By 1961, the NCA was training hundreds of thousands of cheerleaders each year at camps. Cheerleading required athleticism, but at the time it was not competitive. Cheerleaders had become common at high school sports across the country. They also began cheering at other sporting events besides football and basketball. Cheerleading had blossomed into one of the fastest-growing youth activities in the United States.

GETTING COMPETITIVE

In 1964, the International Cheerleading Federation (ICF) was founded. That organization produced the first ratings of college cheerleading teams. Its "Top Ten College Cheer Squads" ranked the best in order in 1967.

▲ *Baltimore Colts cheerleaders salute their team as the players run onto the field before a 1962 game.*

Former NCA executive Jeff Webb took the first step toward competitive cheerleading. Webb founded the Universal Cheerleaders Association (UCA) in 1974. The goal of his organization was to teach advanced skills to cheerleaders across the nation. The UCA believed introducing such skills as **partner stunts** and pyramids would make cheerleaders more entertaining.

The new style of cheerleading first took hold in the southern and central regions of the United States. It soon spread across the country. The UCA continued to create new cheer innovations. One year after it was formed, it began combining music with skills. That created the modern cheerleading routine.

▲ *The famous Dallas Cowboys Cheerleaders perform a dance routine before a home game.*

ICONS

Perhaps no cheerleaders are as identifiable as the Dallas Cowboys Cheerleaders. The NFL team founded the squad in 1972. The cheerleaders impressed millions with their blue and white star-spangled uniforms. They also proved to be talented entertainers. The Dallas Cowboys Cheerleaders are considered the first dance team in professional sports.

The Dallas crowds responded with enthusiasm. And eventually the Cowboys cheerleaders became an American success story. They appeared on two national television shows during the late 1970s. In 1979, *The Dallas Cowboys Cheerleaders* became the highest-rated made-for-TV movie in history. A new TV show called *Dallas Cowboys Cheerleaders: Making the Team* began

Dallas Cowboys Cheerleaders

The Dallas Cowboys Cheerleaders have grown to be international icons. They have made many hundreds of appearances and performed all over the world. They have also done quite a bit to help those in need. They entertain U.S. soldiers overseas and work with organizations seeking cures for various diseases.

on Country Music Television (CMT) in 2006. It followed hopefuls as they auditioned for the team.

NFL cheerleading teams are not just spirit groups. They have also become business departments within their clubs. The cheer teams are often revenue-generating programs. They mentor youth teams, produce halftime productions, feature alumni cheerleader programs, serve as ambassadors for their teams, and travel for military goodwill tours.

CHEERING FOR TROPHIES

By the late 1970s, cheerleading had finally become a competitive activity. In 1978, the ICF launched the annual Collegiate Cheerleading Championships. The event was shown on national television. Competitions were soon launched for middle school and high school cheerleaders as well.

Building the Pyramids

Some of the most popular stunts in competitive cheerleading are pyramids. They can be quite creative. Pyramids are built from the bottom up and one step at a time. The most important part of building a pyramid is to have a strong base. The cheerleaders who rest on top of the base can be organized many different ways. But spotters are required and must be alert at all times. They must catch any teammate who falls from the top. A pyramid is perhaps one of the most dangerous stunts a cheerleading team can perform, along with any **basket toss**.

Cheerleaders no longer represented only boys' and men's sports. By the early 1970s, female athletics had become common in high school and college. So cheerleaders began performing at their sporting events as well.

As skill levels grew in gymnastics, partner stunts, pyramids, and advanced jumps, cheerleaders were starting to be recognized as athletes. Cheerleaders were no longer simply dancing and performing motions on the sidelines. Now they were routinely performing flips and tossing each other high into the air for daring stunts.

While visually captivating, the new moves could be dangerous. If a cheerleader fell or landed awkwardly, she could easily break a bone or suffer from brain injuries. These injuries were often the result of insufficient coaching or certain moves being taught to girls before they were physically prepared to execute them.

Injury prevention has since been a major focus for competitive cheerleading organizations. As the possibility for danger increased, the cheerleading organizations took more steps to certify the instructors and advisers. This ensures that anybody leading a cheerleading team is properly trained. Instructors and advisers were especially important at the middle school and high school levels. The ICF set up a training course for teachers who wished to serve in those jobs. The courses were taught at summer cheerleading camps. Some cheerleading organizations also went as far as to ban moves that were frequently leading to injuries.

OPPORTUNITIES ARISE

Students soon saw a future in cheerleading, and not just as coaches. Universities began offering **scholarships** to high school cheerleaders. Scholarships attract students by helping pay for school. Cheerleaders had gained a reputation throughout the country for working to help others. They became leaders, promoting spirit and a positive attitude in their schools and in their communities. Many do all of this in addition to competing.

By the early 1980s, cable television provided more opportunities to show cheerleading on TV. All-sports network ESPN jumped on board in 1982 by televising the first UCA Cheerleading National Championships. ESPN became the exclusive home of competitive cheerleading. The broadcasts created an interest in cheerleading around the world. Soon it began to take hold in countries such as Canada, the United Kingdom, Mexico, and Finland.

Some were saddened at the growth of cheerleading competition, however. They believed that cheerleading was created to promote school spirit and lead others to cheer. They felt that its original intent had been lost.

Among those who expressed that view was Lawrence "Herkie" Herkimer. He possibly had done more to promote cheerleading than any other person. But he grew concerned with the direction it was going. He believed the new motivation was to form competitive teams rather than to cheer on others.

"I'm amazed cheerleading came so far, so I don't know where it could go from here," he said. "All I can see is it going downhill. If they stop being an asset to the school and to school activities, then cheerleading can die."

Most cheerleaders didn't agree. They felt that cheerleading was as much a sport as football and basketball. It remained what it had been for nearly 100 years—a way to motivate fellow students to cheer. It had also become a competitive activity that required great athletic skill and talent. And it was gaining popularity around the world.

▲ *Cheerleading became more acrobatic as competitive cheerleading grew in popularity during the late 1970s.*

▲ Members of the Marshall High School cheerleading team from Texas compete in the 1995 NCA Cheer National Championships.

CHAPTER 4

THE MODERN ERA

Competitive cheerleading experienced rapid growth in the United States and around the world during the 1980s and 1990s. At the high school level, the UCA and the NCA began holding national cheerleading championships during the early 1980s. Soon college national championships were added as well, and the UCA events were broadcast on television. That helped spur more interest in competitive cheerleading throughout the United States, ultimately leading to more opportunities for young cheerleaders.

The Pop Warner organization held its first youth cheerleading competition in 1988. That was around the same time that All Star cheerleading began, which provided an opportunity for cheerleaders to perform competitively outside of school. Throughout the 1990s, competitive cheerleading on the youth, high school, and college levels grew tremendously. In 1988, there were eight regional or national competitions for these levels. By 2002, there were 62 of them.

The Granny Squad

There were 23 female students at a local high school in Hedrick, Iowa, in 1983. Most of them decided that year to play on the basketball team. That left the school without cheerleaders. So the community recruited six Hedrick grandmothers to lead the cheers that season. They became known as the Granny Squad. They even agreed to continue as the official school cheerleaders the following year.

STAYING SAFE

Since 1974, Jeff Webb had taken the lead in promoting cheerleading. His UCA had expanded it from basketball gyms and football stadiums to the competitive arena.

The result was that cheerleaders performed more difficult and dangerous routines than ever before.

In 1987, Webb founded the American Association of Cheerleading Coaches and Administrators. The new organization established safety standards and taught the standards to cheerleading coaches. It also tested the coaches on what they learned to make sure they understood how to keep their cheerleaders safe.

Cheerleading continued to grow in the United States. The National Federation of High School Associations reported in 1990 that 1.7 million students were participating. The tremendous interest in the sport was helped by the emergence of All Star cheerleading.

Dangerous Activity

Parents have reason to worry about their kids who compete in cheerleading. A 1999 study by the National Center for Catastrophic Sport Injury Research explained why. The study looked mainly at head and neck injuries from 1982 to 1999. It noted that cheerleaders suffered nearly 50 percent of all serious head and neck injuries to female high school athletes. At the college level, where stunts are more dangerous, the figure rose to a frightening 76.3 percent. Though few female athletes died while participating in a sport during that time, about half who were killed were cheerleaders.

▲ *With high flying, acrobatic moves such as this one, cheerleading developed into an exciting but potentially dangerous sport.*

All Star cheerleading led the way for bringing more gymnastics skills into competitive cheerleading. All Star teams focused more on acrobatic stunts and tumbling than many school teams. As such, male cheerleaders returned to prominence at the most advanced levels. They were needed for their strength in throwing and catching their teammates.

GOING GLOBAL

As cheerleading grew in the United States and competitions were broadcast on ESPN, it also became more popular around the world. Webb and his UCA first took cheerleading to Japan in 1988. A group from Japan asked Webb and his organization to teach cheerleading to the youth of that country. The UCA accepted. Soon it operated training camps throughout Japan. It also helped the country organize cheerleading competitions.

The sport also blossomed in England. The UCA sent a group of cheerleaders to perform in the 1989 New Year's Day Parade in London, England. That introduced cheerleading to many new people and inspired many in that country to begin cheering themselves. Since then, U.S. and other international cheerleaders have performed every year at the event in front of thousands of people.

The UCA was just warming up. The organization introduced cheerleading to Austria, France, and Ireland in 1992. U.S. cheerleaders participated that year in New

▲ *U.S. cheerleaders perform in front of Big Ben during the 2007 New Year's Day Parade in London, England.*

▲ *This cheerleader performs a lift during an American football game in Germany.*

Year's Day celebrations in the cities of Paris, France, and Vienna, Austria. That helped spur more growth of cheerleading among Europeans.

But where would these new European cheerleaders perform? Soccer, or football as most Europeans know it, did not have cheerleaders. But the growing popularity of American gridiron football provided an opportunity.

In 1991, the new World League of American Football (WLAF) placed teams in several European cities. Cheerleading grew in popularity on that continent. So did the cheerleaders who represented those teams.

Author Mary Ellen Hanson wrote about WLAF cheerleaders in her 1995 book *Go! Fight! Win!: Cheerleading in American Culture*. Each team had a unique name for their cheerleading squad. Hanson referred to a feature aired on the TV show *Entertainment Tonight*:

> *The Barcelona [Spain] Dragon Girls were said to be "celebrities in their own right." The London Monarch Crown Jewels performed in a soccer stadium behind a wire barrier between the field and the stands; and the Frankfurt [Germany] squad, which had an English choreographer, cheered in English and German.*

Competitive cheerleading in Europe received a major boost in 1994 when the European Cheerleading Association (ECA) was formed. It promotes cheerleading

Paula Abdul began her show business career as a Laker Girl.

A CHEERLEADING IDOL

Paula Abdul tried out for the Laker Girls cheerleading squad in 1980. She not only made the team, but she was quickly named head cheerleader. She later served as the Laker Girls' choreographer. Abdul's singing career took off soon after. Her first album sold 12 million copies and boasted four singles that reached the top of the charts. Abdul also gained fame as a judge on the hit reality TV show American Idol.

and organizes competition throughout Europe. In 2011, the ECA boasted membership from 17 countries.

NBA CHEERLEADERS

By the 1990s, many NFL cheer teams were moving away from stunt cheerleading. Performing outside, sometimes in cold weather, made it too dangerous. Some NFL teams have continued on without them. The NFL's Green Bay Packers, rather than having their own team, invite a local college cheerleading team to lead crowds at their home games.

Cold weather was not a problem for NBA cheerleaders, who performed indoors. The NBA cheerleaders could perform dance and gymnastic routines that couldn't be done as effectively or as safely on outdoor football fields.

▲ *The Laker Girls, who cheer for the Los Angeles Lakers, are the most famous NBA cheerleaders.*

However, like most NFL cheerleaders, the NBA performers have become mainly dancers today. The most famous NBA cheerleaders represent the Los Angeles Lakers. The Laker Girls soon rivaled the Dallas Cowboys Cheerleaders in overall popularity. By 2006, every NBA team had cheerleaders.

▲ *Competitive cheerleading has continued to grow in popularity since the 1970s.*

CHAPTER 5

CHEERING FOR CHAMPIONSHIPS

Cheerleaders continue to support many high school and college sports teams on the sidelines. But by the early 2000s, competitive cheerleading had taken center stage. And there are more opportunities for cheerleaders today than there ever have been before.

Through organizations such as American Youth Cheer (AYC), NCA, UCA, and the All Star program, youth can begin cheerleading as early as age five. College and high school cheerleaders often work double duty, cheering for their school's teams while also competing. There are even opportunities for beginner cheerleaders to cheer for youth football teams while also competing. All Star teams, however, focus solely on competitive cheerleading.

Still, not all cheerleaders start at young ages. Many competitive cheerleaders only begin when they join a high school squad. Prior to that, many prepare for the dynamic world of competitive cheerleading through other sports, such as gymnastics or dance.

Explosion of Popularity

The growth of cheerleading in the 1990s and beyond wasn't just seen at sporting events and camps. It was evident through media attention as well. A new magazine about cheerleading called *American Cheerleader* hit the market in 1994. It had 1.2 million readers by 2010. In addition, a movie about cheerleading titled *Bring it On* was a hit in 2000.

Cheerleading camps are also a great way for aspiring cheerleaders to get involved. The various cheerleading organizations, as well as individual teams, put on these camps all across the United States. Some are geared toward beginners looking to learn the basics and make some friends. More advanced cheerleaders can go to

▲ *Cheerleading camps, such as this one in Wisconsin, are a great way to learn new skills.*

camps and learn new moves to perform with their teams. Either way, these camps have become a popular destination for thousands of cheerleaders each summer.

CREATING A ROUTINE

The performance is the most exciting part of cheerleading. Teams get to show off their synchronized movements, athletic jumps, and acrobatic stunts and tumbling passes. With an upbeat song blasting over the speakers and an energetic crowd to feed off, there is nothing like performing.

But while performing is great, a typical routine only lasts around two-and-a-half minutes. Yet hours and hours of practice go into creating and perfecting the routine. That time spent working with your teammates to develop and perfect a routine makes the journey worth it.

When creating a routine, the first step is assessing the strengths and weaknesses of your team. For example, if your team has great tumblers, you might want to focus on doing more advanced tumbling moves. Once you've decided the overall direction, it's time to pick the music for your routine. The music is key to any performance. Many of your moves and transitions will be timed to go along with the beats and transitions in the song. Likewise, a high-energy, upbeat song helps energize the team and the crowd.

Once you have a song, it's time to map out the choreography, or exactly what everybody will be doing during your routine. This is a very important but difficult step, so many teams work with a professional choreographer to help them. Some teams even dedicate a few days at a cheerleading camp as the time to choreograph their routine.

Each routine includes many different parts. It will have dancing, tumbling, stunting, motions, and jumping all in a short time period. The key is developing a routine that flows so you can transition from one stage to the next in a smooth way. Matching the various moves to the music is also important.

▲ *These cheerleaders practice for a high school cheerleading competition in North Carolina.*

PRACTICE MAKES PERFECT

Creating a routine is one thing; mastering it is a whole new challenge. You and your team will likely spend hours upon hours practicing your routine over several weeks. Some of the work will be on personal execution. The team is judged on individual precision. So, for example, on jumps you'll want to make sure your legs get high and your toes are pointed. No matter what, executing moves is very important. And it is better to perform easier moves well than harder moves poorly.

Varsity Spirit

In 2004, the NCA and the UCA became a part of Varsity Spirit, a major cheerleading organization that runs camps and clinics while also selling cheerleading gear. Both the NCA and the UCA still exist within Varsity Spirit and run their own competitions, including their own major high school and college national events.

There are differences between the styles of cheerleading promoted by the UCA and NCA. Those contrasts can be seen in the national events run by both organizations. University of Alabama cheerleading coach Rebecca Grier has strong opinions about those differences. "The UCA teaches more about game cheerleading and the ability to lead the crowd in a game," she said. "The NCA is more All Star cheerleading. It's more glittery and showy."

You'll also be judged on team execution, such as synchronization, transitions, and stunts. It takes a lot of hard work to get these down just right. But when the competition comes, it will all be worth it when your team performs as one cohesive unit on the floor. And plus, the teamwork and practice that comes before the competition is a huge part of what makes cheerleading great!

CHEERING IN COLLEGE

Some of the most high profile and exciting competitive cheerleading is done by college teams. Most of the biggest and best cheerleading teams compete in the UCA championships. Among them is the University of Kentucky, which has dominated the event. The cheerleaders there have done more than lead cheers for one of the finest basketball teams in the country. They have also won the UCA College Cheerleading National Championships nearly every year.

The Kentucky squad has captured 18 national titles through 2011. That includes eight in a row from 1995 to 2002. Kentucky is the only team to ever win more than three in a row. Only an upset victory by Alabama in 2011 prevented Kentucky from extending its latest streak to four.

Kentucky coach Jomo K. Thompson said that some of the best high school cheerleaders are attracted to his school. One reason is that it gives them a chance to cheer

▲ University of Kentucky cheerleaders and their mascot (on top) perform a pyramid during one of the school's men's basketball games in 2010.

for big crowds at the school's football and basketball games. But the same could be said for cheerleaders at other universities. So why has Kentucky won most of the UCA events?

"It's a dedication to excellence," Thompson said. "We start by taking people who fit the mold we're looking for. We look for people who are talented, have personality and a great work ethic. Our coaches don't settle for anything less than hard work in every practice and an attention to detail."

Kentucky and Alabama are often among the best cheerleading universities in the nation. They are just two of the many top universities from the Southeast, though. Many of the top competitive squads at both the high school and college levels come from that area of the country.

Spirit Stick

One of the most exciting parts of a cheerleading camp is at the end, when the instructors hand out awards to the campers. Perhaps the most anticipated award is the spirit stick, which is given out to the team that has shown the most spirit throughout camp. The tradition started at an NCA camp during the 1950s. Spirit sticks can be made out of anything, from a small piece of wood to the cardboard from the inside of a roll of paper towels.

In the 2011 UCA championships, eight of the first 11 finishers were from the Southeast. The top four were Alabama, Kentucky, Central Florida, and Louisiana State. It's no wonder that summer cheerleading camps are more popular in the Southeast than in any other part of the United States.

Cheerleaders throughout the nation have embraced competition in recent years. Liana Sheintal cheered for George Washington University in Washington D.C. She had become used to leading the cheers for the basketball team. Then she was leading the cheers to try to win championships for her own cheerleading squad as well. "We're always cheering for them," she said. "This is the one time we get to cheer for us."

WORLD CHAMPIONS

Top cheerleading competition isn't limited to schools and professional sports teams. The International Cheer Union (ICU) also hosts the World Cheerleading Championships each year for national cheerleading teams. The teams, which are made up of citizens of a respective country, compete in 12 different cheering categories. At least one country from every continent except Antarctica competed in the 2011 event.

Another group, the United States All Star Federation (USASF) also holds a world championship event called the Cheerleading Worlds. This event began in 2004 and is shown on ESPN. It includes the top All Star teams from cheerleading gyms around the world.

TITLE IX

In 1972, the U.S. government passed Title IX. It required any program or activity that received federal funding to give equal opportunities to men and women. Today, most people know of Title IX because of its effect on sports. Since the law went into place, opportunities and participation in high school and college women's sports has skyrocketed.

Cheerleading has not gotten the same benefits as other sports. That's because, according to a U.S. District Judge in 2010, cheerleading isn't a sport. Although cheerleading is filled with athletic and acrobatic moves, the judge determined that, among other things, the competitive structure did not match other sports and that cheerleading was "too underdeveloped and disorganized."

Two groups are trying to change that. In 2010, USA Gymnastics and USA Cheer submitted proposals to the National Collegiate Athletic Association (NCAA) to make cheerleading an "emerging sport." That is the first step toward making it an official NCAA sport. Should that happen, college cheerleading teams would count under Title IX and could see increased funding and also more scholarship opportunities. An official NCAA championship would also be created.

▲ *The future is bright for cheerleaders such as these from the University of Alabama.*

Cheerleading has come a long way since it began in the late 1800s. With exciting acrobatics, tumbling, and stunts, cheerleading performances continue to find new and amazing ways to entertain and energize crowds. And whether it's school or All Star squads, more people are cheerleading around the world than ever before. It's time to get out there and cheer!

GLOSSARY

basket toss: A stunt in which two or more bases toss a flyer into the air and then catch her by interlocking their hands like a basket. The flyer often performs a trick while in the air.

chants: Short yells that are repeated.

cheers: Long, spirited yells generally performed during breaks in a game and often used with a variety of motions.

cradle: The end move when a base (or bases) catch a flyer after a stunt.

flyers: The cheerleaders sent into the air during a stunt.

jumps: When cheerleaders spring into the air with both feet leaving the ground.

megaphone: An instrument used to better project the voice of a cheerleader into the stands.

motions: Movements such as those done by the arms, legs, and hands during a cheer or chant.

partner stunts: Stunts involving multiple teammates that begin with a toss.

pep club: A group of students who bring energy to a team by cheering or playing music during games. Cheerleading developed out of one of these clubs in the 1880s.

pompoms: Hand-held props that add visual effect to cheer motions.

pyramid: A stunt with one or more flyers supported by one or more bases on a team.

routines: Series of choreographed moves used by cheerleaders.

scholarships: Money given to students to help them pay for classes or other college expenses as a reward for skills in specific areas, such as cheerleading.

stunts: Any routines that include tumbling, tossing, or the creation of a pyramid.

tucks: Flips done in a tuck position, forwards, or backwards. The tuck position involves pulling the knees and legs tight to the chest so the cheerleader can flip faster. Tucks can be done within a tumbling pass or alone.

tumbling passes: A series of connected gymnastic skills used in cheerleading.

FOR MORE INFORMATION

BOOKS

Golden, Suzi. *101 Best Cheers*. New York: Troll Communications, 2001.
This book teaches readers how to do popular cheers used by high school and college cheerleaders.

Guice Adams, Natalie, and Pamela Bettis. *Cheerleader! An American Icon*. New York: Palgrave Macmillan, 2003.
This book is an in-depth look at the role of cheerleading in American society.

Inside Cheerleading Magazine. *Cheerleading From Tryouts to Championships*. New York: Universe, 2007.
This book introduces all aspects of competitive cheerleading to beginners. Topics include the sport's history, cheerleading camps, team tryouts and practices, uniforms, and major competitions.

Peters, Craig. *Competitive Cheerleading*. Philadelphia: Mason Crest Publishers, 2003.
This book discusses the history of cheerleading and offers instructions and tips for improving.

Wilson, Leslie. *The Ultimate Guide to Cheerleading: For Cheerleaders and Coaches*. New York: Three Rivers Press, 2003.
This book, written for beginners or those with experience, has step-by-step guides, training tips, safety information, and other information about finding success in cheerleading.

WEBSITES

American Cheerleader
www.americancheerleader.com
This official *American Cheerleader* magazine website features blogs and articles about cheerleading and also has videos.

American Youth Football & Cheer
www.americanyouthfootball.com/cheerleading.asp
The official website for American Youth Cheer has information about youth cheerleading and how to get involved.

Kidzworld.com
www.kidzworld.com/article/2492-cheerleading-tips
This website gives tips about how to become the best cheerleader possible.

Varsity
www.varsity.com
This official Varsity.com website provides information about cheerleading camps and competitions. Visitors can also see videos of cheerleading routines and stunts.

INDEX

PLACES TO VISIT

ESPN Wide World of Sports Complex

700 S. Victory Way, Kissimmee, FL 34747
www.espnwwos.disney.go.com
This complex, which is part of Disney World, is home to
several cheerleading events each year, such as the UCA/UDA
College Cheerleading and Dance Team Championship and
the Pop Warner National Cheer and Dance Championships.
Cheerleading is hardly the only sport to compete here. The
Wide World of Sports Complex is host to more than 200
sporting events each year. It has facilities to host 60 different
sports in its nine venues.

ABOUT THE AUTHOR

Marty Gitlin is a freelance writer based in
Cleveland, Ohio. He has written more than 40
educational books. Gitlin has won more than 45
awards during his 25 years as a writer, including
first place for general excellence from the
Associated Press. He lives with his wife and
three children.

ABOUT THE CONTENT CONSULTANT

Tami Krause is the Head Coach/Coordinator for
the Minnesota Vikings Cheerleaders (NFL) and
the Minnesota Swarm (NLL) Performance Team.
She has a bachelor's degree in dance from the
University of Minnesota and coached competitively
to five state championships and choreographed
two National College Championships. She has
been a certified dance and cheer judge locally, nationally, and
internationally and is in the UPA Hall of Fame.